The Wonderful Life of MR. BEAR

Written by Patrice Maguire
Illustrated by Gail Lloyd

The Wonderful Life of Mr. Bear
Copyright © 2019—Patrice Maguire
ALL RIGHTS RESERVED UNDER U.S., PAN-AMERICAN AND INTERNATIONAL COPYRIGHTS.
No part of this publication may be reproduced, stored in a retrieval system or transmitted in any form by mechanical, electronic, photocopying, recording or otherwise without the prior written consent of the author.

Published by:

Little Oaks Publishing
18896 Greenwell Springs Road
Greenwell Springs, LA 70739
www.thepublishedword.com

ISBN: 978-1-940461-43-4 Trade paper version
978-1-940461-49-6 Casebound version

Printed on demand
For Worldwide Distribution

This book

is dedicated

to the

memory

of

Mr. Bear

There once was a puppy named Mr. Bear. He was very smart, and he looked like a baby polar bear. Mr. Bear had fluffy white hair, with one small patch of light yellow hair on his back. He was so cute and cuddly.

When Mr. Bear was old enough, he was sent to doggy school. He was trained very well. He became even smarter than before, and he learned many good manners.

Mr. Bear was the proud puppy of a truck driver. Together they traveled all over the country. Looking through the window, Mr. Bear would see many interesting sights.

While on their journeys, he and the truck driver would visit a lot of truck stops. Mr. Bear enjoyed meeting new people and being petted by them. Everyone loved Mr. Bear, especially the truck driver.

Mr. Bear and the truck driver happily traveled around the country for many years. Truck driving was the only life they knew. When they were home, the truck driver only had time to rest and run errands.

The truck driver never had time to teach Mr. Bear how to play. Mr. Bear only knew how to go for rides and how to be cute and loveable. While they traveled, the truck driver would pet Mr. Bear as he lay in his lap. Mr. Bear loved being petted. He had a wonderful life.

One day, while traveling, something terrible happened to the truck driver. He got very sick and had to stop his truck on the side of the road. He called 911 because he needed an ambulance. The police came to help.

Mr. Bear was very confused. He could sense that something was wrong with the truck driver, but he didn't know what it was. Mr. Bear cried. The ambulance came and took the truck driver away, and the police took Mr. Bear with them in their car.

Mr. Bear was very sad. He had been with the truck driver his whole life. Now the truck driver was gone, and Mr. Bear was all alone in the world. He didn't know where he was going or if he'd ever see the truck driver again. He loved and missed the truck driver very much.

The police took Mr. Bear to a pet adoption agency in a nearby town. There were a lot of other dogs and cats there. The people there were very friendly, and Mr. Bear felt safe. They took good care of him. Sometimes, when they weren't busy, they would pet him.

The people took his picture and put it on their pet adoption website, with a short description of him. Mr. Bear was now up for adoption.

One day a young boy decided he was ready to have a pet. He went on the Internet to find the perfect dog. He saw a picture of Mr. Bear and fell in love with him. The boy showed the picture of the dog to his mom. The mom saw that Mr. Bear cost $200.00. She told the boy that he could have Mr. Bear if he could pay the adoption fee. So the boy made a plan.

There was going to be a festival in their town soon, so the boy decided he was going to sell lemonade to earn money to buy Mr. Bear. He printed out the picture of Mr. Bear from the adoption website and made a sign that read, "Help me adopt a pet."

On the morning of the festival, the boy set up his table next to the road in front of his house with the picture of Mr. Bear and the sign. He made the lemonade, set it on the table and waited for the money to pour in to adopt Mr. Bear.

Many people bought lemonade, but some just gave donations to help the boy adopt Mr. Bear. By the end of the festival, he had earned $50.00.

The boy was very sad because he didn't have enough money to pay the adoption fee. He asked his mom to loan him the rest of the money he needed to adopt Mr. Bear. He promised to pay her back with his weekly allowance. His mom agreed. This made the boy very happy!

The next day the boy and his mom contacted the pet adoption agency, making arrangements to adopt Mr. Bear. Mr. Bear was two hours away in another town. Because the boy had school that week, he would have to wait until the weekend before traveling to adopt Mr. Bear. The boy was overwhelmed with excitement!

Saturday morning the boy and his family traveled the two hours to adopt Mr. Bear. When they arrived at the pet adoption agency, Mom and Dad filled out the paperwork and paid the $200.00 adoption fee. Meanwhile, the boy and his brothers were visiting with Mr. Bear. Mr. Bear was so happy to have their attention. Once all the paperwork was completed, they were ready to head home.

Mr. Bear excitedly jumped into the back seat of the car. He was so happy to go for a ride again. He had missed traveling with the truck driver. Now he was on the road again, and he loved every minute of it. The boy was happy too. He finally had his pet dog and couldn't wait to get home to start their new life together as best pals.

The boy and Mr. Bear had many good times together. Mr. Bear would sleep with the boy in his bed. He fed him, gave him fresh water, and brushed him every day. They would even go for walks together.

The boy tried to teach Mr. Bear how to play, but Mr. Bear wasn't interested. Mr. Bear's favorite thing to do was to lie with the boy and be petted by him.

When the boy would return home from school, they would lie on the floor together and take a nap. Mr. Bear was so happy to have someone to love him again.

Then came the time for Mr. Bear and his family to move. They had been living where the weather was cold, but now they were moving to where it was warm.

Mr. Bear preferred the colder temperatures. He had thick fluffy hair to keep him warm. Plus, he enjoyed running around in the snow. But he didn't mind the move or warmer temperatures much, as long as he was with the boy. Mr. Bear and the boy were inseparable.

Mr. Bear was happy in his new home. The boy's new bedroom was upstairs. As Mr. Bear grew older, it became harder for him to get up and down the stairs. He couldn't jump up into the boy's bed like he used to, so the boy had to help him. Mr. Bear was getting old, and this made the boy and his family very sad. They wanted to enjoy Mr. Bear for as long as they could.

When they moved into their new home, the boy and his family adopted two more pets: a cat named Miela and a dog named Autumn. Mr. Bear liked chasing Miela and Autumn around the backyard. He didn't mind the new pets, as long as he still got most of the attention from the boy.

As Mr. Bear got older, his health grew worse. He couldn't go for walks anymore, and he was losing his eyesight and hearing. Mr. Bear loved to eat, but he wasn't able to enjoy his food. He had lost a lot of his teeth, and he was having trouble chewing and swallowing. It was very sad for the boy and his family to watch Mr. Bear's health decline. They didn't want to imagine their lives without him.

The boy and his parents took Mr. Bear to the animal doctor many times to try to make him better, but eventually the doctors ran out of ways to help Mr. Bear. The boy was so sad that he felt as though his heart was breaking the day Mr. Bear passed away. He had never known such sadness before that moment. The boy and his family cried. The boy knew that this day would come, but when it did come, he wasn't ready to say good-bye to his best friend.

Mr. Bear was fifteen years old when he passed away, surrounded by his boy and his family. Many people loved Mr. Bear, and he loved many people. He will forever live in their hearts and memories. Mr. Bear had a lot of good times and some not-so-good times. But, all in all, he lived a wonderful life.

The End

Considering Sadness

In the story, Mr. Bear was sad when the truck driver got sick and had to go away. He was sad that he never got to see the truck driver again. The boy was sad when he thought things wouldn't work out for him to adopt Mr. Bear. He and his family were sad when Mr. Bear was sick and couldn't enjoy his life as he had before, when he was young and healthy. And they were even sadder when he passed away.

Do you sometimes get sad? What are some things that make you sad? Maybe the things that make you sad are similar to the things that made Mr. Bear and his family sad. Mr. Bear and his family cried when they were sad. It's okay to cry when you are sad. Even Jesus cried when He was sad (John 11:35).

God's Word says, in Psalm 34:18, that God is close to the brokenhearted and helps those who are sad. You can ask God to comfort you and help you to not be so sad.

First, on the page titled "Things I Am Sad About," you can write down what makes you sad, with the date. Then, on the page titled "Answers To Prayer," you can write how God is helping you and answering your prayers, with the date. Maybe your mom and dad can help you. As you see God answering your prayers, your faith will grow, and you will learn to trust God more and more to heal your broken heart.

Let's pray:

Dear God,
Your Word says that You are close to those who have a broken heart and that You help those who are sad. Please help me not to be sad about _____ (this is where you name what is making you sad from your list). Heal my broken heart. Help me to focus on things that make me happy. Help me to trust You and know that You are close to me. Thank You, God. In Jesus' name I pray. Amen!

Things I Am Sad About

Answers to Prayer

Mr. Bear was the type of dog that had to be groomed regularly. He was an American Eskimo. Every visit to the groomer he would get a neckerchief to wear home. He was so handsome in his little neckerchiefs! We kept all of them over the course of Mr. Bear's life.

For Christmas 2016, my husband and I had a quilt made with all of the neckerchiefs that we had collected, and we gave it to our son (the boy in the story) as a Christmas gift. He cherishes it. He is in the military now and keeps it with him as a reminder of the special bond he shared with his best friend, Mr. Bear.

I hope you have enjoyed this story about the wonderful life of Mr. Bear and that it inspires you to go to God with your sadness, to trust Him to heal your broken heart, and to focus on things that make you happy.

Patrice Maguire

If you enjoyed this Little Oaks book by Patrice Maguire, look for:

The Many Fears of Miela the Cat.

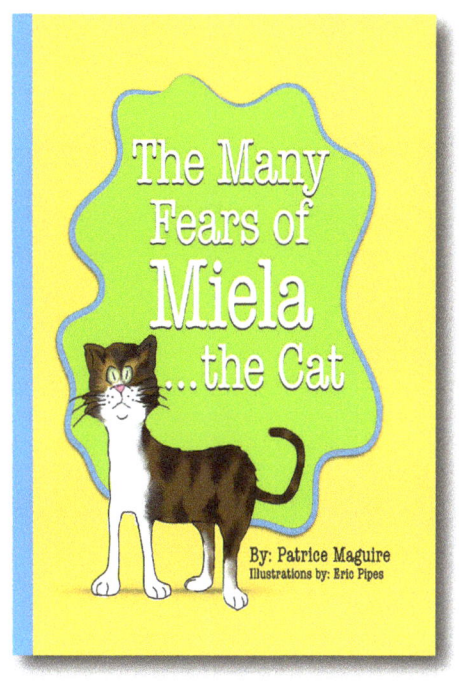

www.ingramcontent.com/pod-product-compliance
Lightning Source LLC
LaVergne TN
LVHW070837080426
835510LV00026B/3421